MEN WHO MATTER

MEN WHO MATTER

COMPILED BY RUTH L. SNYDER &
SHEILA WEBSTER

Copyright © 2023 by RLS Creativity

All rights reserved.

No part of this book may be reproduced in any form or by any electronic or mechanical means, including information storage and retrieval systems, without written permission from the author, except for the use of brief quotations in a book review.

E-book ISBN: 978-1-7771313-8-8

Paperback ISBN: 978-1-7771313-7-1

CONTENTS

1. The Best Man in Town — 1
   By Dallas - age 10
2. For Better or Worse — 3
   By Carol Harrison
3. My Grandpa — 11
   By Sophie Beam
4. My Dad — 15
   By Sheila Mansell
5. Dad by Choice — 19
   By Tandy Balson
6. A Godly Father's Prayers — 23
   By Duane Sims
7. How My Veteran Loves — 27
   By Deacon Minister Sharlae Harris
8. Walter Kittler — 35
   By Sheila Webster
9. My Adopted Brother — 39
   By Mary Anne Focht
10. My Best Friend — 41
    By Sheila Webster
11. More than Reading, Writing, and Arithmetic — 47
    By Ruth L. Snyder
12. The Company of Men — 53
    By Sheila Webster
13. My Dad Was Always There for Me — 57
    By Ashley Carroll
14. My Teacher — 63
    By Zander Bradley - Age 16

15. **Men I Admire** *By Luke Snyder*	67
16. **Todd Magnus** *By Mary Anne Focht*	69
17. **It's How You Finish** *By Tracy Krauss*	73
18. **Mitch Osiowy**	81
19. **Three Men I Admire** *By Joshua Heath*	87
20. **A Husband of Character** *By Sally Meadows*	91
21. **Josia** *By Sheila Webster*	99
22. **Things I Like to Do with My Dad** *By Dane - Age 5*	103
23. **A Father of Many Talents** *By Jewell VanStone*	105
24. **Joel** *By Ares - age 7*	113
25. **A Heart Son** *By Sheila Webster*	117
26. **My Memories of Dad** *By Ruth L. Snyder*	121
27. **Clark Deacon** *By Sheila Webster*	131
28. **Grandpappa** *Tessie - age 5*	135
29. **Cor Hartenberg** *By Sheila Sims*	139
Books Compiled by Ruth L. Snyder & Sheila Webster	143

DEDICATION

We gratefully dedicate this book to the man who donated money to InScribe over many years for the Barnabas Award.

This visionary man left a legacy amongst many InScribers by giving enough money for an award of $250 dollars each year.

This award helped many recipients realize goals and dreams in their writing pursuits, along with encouraging them.

As well, this award impacted all the readers of those writers.

He was also faithful and humble wanting to forever remain anonymous to the recipients and Public alike.

May more men, such as this one, bestow on other organizations like-minded awards, gifts, or scholarships.

1

THE BEST MAN IN TOWN

BY DALLAS - AGE 10

I live in a small town where there are lots of men around. Most of them don't see me.

But one does. His name makes me smile and I want to be like him because he is kind.

He is also funny and teaches me things. Even though I don't like cold I wanted to go when he taught me to snowboard. I went like a million times because I wanted him to be proud of me for trying instead of crying about how cold it was.

One time on my birthday the only thing I wanted was to go for supper with him and Aunty.

It was the most special birthday ever! We went to Boston Pizza, and I remember feeling amazing and focused. He talked to me and Aunty, we laughed, ate, and talked.

He was kind to us and paid too! Even though that was two years ago every time I think about it, I feel spectacular.

Then we had so much fun too. He made Aunty play basketball with us in the dark even though it was raining.

We made Aunty play monkey in the middle and we won against her.

Our fingers were freezing, but inside I felt warm and happy.

He also gave me the basketball for my birthday. It was black and yellow. I will never forget that birthday even if I live to be a million!

2

FOR BETTER OR WORSE

BY CAROL HARRISON

On a hot summer day in 1974, my prince charming and I stood before family, friends, and God to say our vows. Young, starry-eyed and in love, we repeated those beautiful words. His promise to me, that day, was to love, honor, and cherish me for better or worse, richer or poorer, in sickness and health until death parted us. What would that look like in everyday life, moving forward?

We knew happily ever after, this side of heaven, only existed in fairy tales and Hallmark movies. Yet we thought the dragons wouldn't need conquering or those with evil intentions would leave us alone. In other words, we didn't want to think about the worst-case scenarios, the sickness, or even the state of our finances. After all, we had just finished university with no money in the bank. Things had to look up from here, didn't they?

Young, healthy, strong, hard-working, and feeling invincible all described my husband, Brian. Let's not forget handsome (in my opinion) and definitely a tease from the time I dared to talk to him.

Communication was always a strong point in our relationship. We talked about everything and anything from the time we started dating. If distance separated us, we wrote letters filled with everyday life happenings, dreams for the future, and even the tough stuff in our lives. Mine had been like a picnic in the park compared to his.

Brian learned about grief at the early age of three when his dad died in an accident. A stepfather and more siblings added positive things to his life but by the time he turned ten, his three-year-old brother had died in a farming accident. Life became difficult with many arguments between his parents in their time of grief.

As Brian watched the family dynamics, the bitterness, and the continued unresolved grieving, mixed in with hard work and fun times too, he made a choice to be different when he grew up and found the girl he'd marry. He planned to love and cherish his wife no matter what the circumstances, rather than let hard times pull them apart.

Tough stuff marched into our lives uninvited and unwelcomed. The better days faded into the background, but Brian chose to have us work together, continue communicating, praying, and weathering the storms as a united front. He tried to protect me whenever he could.

For richer or poorer, we chuckled as we promised that since poorer existed in our life when we married. Throughout the years, Brian showed his love in tangible ways of working hard and striving to provide the best he could for our growing family. But he also had a hard time saying no to others who might need help or a place to stay and our home had a revolving door at times of family and friends' kids staying for a night or week, a month or multiple years. Richer never showed up. Poorer got more prevalent as we started over financially on more than one occasion.

In sickness and health had to be dealt with multiple times through the years. He never seemed to be the one to get sick—at least not with the usual culprits like the flu or colds. He never needed surgery or broke bones but I did. Brian would look after me, help me, and worry about me too. He'd laugh at himself and say, "It's a good thing I'm like a rubber ball. I fall and bounce right back up, ready to go again."

In the last couple of years, we have both been so grateful for that rubber ball body of his because he's had a few serious falls. If it had been me with those falls, I would have broken something for sure.

Health can be fragile. The hardest times we've had in our married life have been when his cancer returned for a second go round. We investigated multiple types of treatment with the same result. He wasn't a candidate for it. He had to quit the job he loved. He grieved what he could no longer do that had been part of his daily life. He questioned God about why He allowed this to happen. Brian even went through a dark time of trying to push everyone away to protect them from watching his pain.

But I reminded him of those vows which said in sickness and health; for better or worse. We'd do what we always did and stick together through whatever was and is still to come. It took time, prayers, and persistence to keep the channels of communication open. We needed to pull together like never before. It hasn't been easy and has taken a lot of work.

Throughout the years of our marriage, I watched and felt Brian honor, love and cherish me, but also how he dealt honestly and fairly with others. He often went out of his way to help someone, listen to them, or even lend them some money when we didn't know if it would be returned. When he trained people to drive semi trucks, he took the students that struggled and found ways to help them understand what was being taught. He never gave up on them.

Brian never gave up on me either. He's kept all those promises he'd made on our wedding day. His work ethic caused missed family time as he showed his love for us in the tangible way he knew. He provided the best he could for us. The decreasing ability to enjoy activities he's always done and the increase in pain have left him a lot of time to think. He tells everyone not to put off doing things on your bucket list because you never know if you'll have later to do it. He's also had time to take trips down memory lane. At night, after the house is quiet, we talk and share like has been our habit. So many memoires have been shared in the last couple of years, including the good, the bad, and the ugly ones too.

I have always known through his words and actions, how deeply he loved me just the way I was right then, no matter what. He's never tried to change me and always encourages me. He often believes I can accomplish things I'm not sure I can. There have been many high points and low ones too. The one constant during our marriage has been his love and care.

We meant those vows decades ago when life looked great. They have a deeper meaning today after dealing with financial issues, health problems, and the threat of cancer taking him earlier than we want. No matter the twists and turns, the ups and downs of life, and the unknowns of the present situation with comfort care only for him, Brian has demonstrated his love, encouragement, and kept communication central in our relationship. He's not perfect by any means but neither am I. But those difficult times have drawn us closer together, needing to rely on God more and more, and given us opportunities to extend forgiveness and grace to each other. I count it a rich blessing to watch him deal honorably with everyone he encounters. I'm richer, not in dollars and cents, but in how I've been loved and cherished for almost five decades.

3

MY GRANDPA

BY SOPHIE BEAM

Basically, my grandpa was amazing when we visited him which was once every two years. Now, I have Cerebral Palsy which means that I am in a wheelchair most of the time and it made it very difficult for me to sit on any one's lap. However, Grandpa would hold me and we just chilled. Sometimes with his dog Pal as well, which I loved.

MY GRANDPA

The picture on the back of this book is me and Grandpa. He is walking, holding my hand while I was driving my first ever power chair down the road. Back then I was probably 12 years old. The driving system was slow as I had to wait for the scanner to scan to the direction that I wanted to go then press the button which I did with my head. That is a good memory of my grandpa.

Sophie's Dad explains how Sophie wrote this submission:

Sophie types by looking at each key she wants to type. The eye tracker on her communication computer interprets a long enough pause as a key press and offers her predictive text words she can choose from or she can keep spelling on the keyboard. It's tedious and slow, but effective.

4

MY DAD

BY SHEILA MANSELL

I remember thinking what an interesting name Mansell was when I was young, before I knew that last names in the beginning were to differentiate people's families. (Johnson was John's son.)

I thought it was interesting that my dad sold furnaces - so he was a man that sells.

I was born into the family knowing my dad was a hard worker. He took care of his brothers and sisters and mom — as well as helping my mom's parents and having us.

He tried to laugh and have fun through jokes and stories and things.

My mom and dad had lots of family and friends, and church people as well as business clients coming for visits or meals in our one-bedroom home which housed six people.

Dad would often be gone long days working at a business he owned with several partners. J&S Heating (1967 inc. I think.)

In the beginning it was the most common initials of the business partners; in the end as he was the last one standing it appeared to represent my parents' initials, Janice & Stan, as my mom provided his bookkeeping and call service. My dad would joke it stood for junk and stuff as he owned many of his original tools.

My parents never would have built the new house in the eighties if the city hadn't insisted on building our riverbank property up to being one of the better places to live. For most of their married life they have lived in the same area of Red Deer but just two lots over from their original home.

My dad supplied us with lots of fun gadgets like dirt bikes, three-wheelers, old vehicles, snowmobiles — gifted to us by those who couldn't pay their bills.

My dad also tried to give us mini breaks. We went to the lake occasionally, fishing from the bank of the river, family reunions and a larger trip once to see the coast and a bit of the Washington State area where my mom's dad was from.

My dad probably had his own hopes and dreams — maybe a coffee shop, less work, less stress over bills or us kids growing up. He, however, still works part time at 85. "Has to help out the old people," he says.

He taught us all to go to church, work hard, not complain, help less fortunate, put family first, don't share your troubles with others, listen to others, and take a little time off to relax.

5

DAD BY CHOICE

BY TANDY BALSON

I've heard it said that anyone can be a father, but it takes someone special to be a dad. My son-in-law, Lucas, is a perfect example of that someone special.

When he met my daughter, she was the mother of two young girls. He soon fell in love with all three of them. Less than a year later, a wedding took place, and they became a family.

As the girls grew, he was there to instruct and watch over them. They were nourished, cared for and disciplined when necessary. He loved his children. They loved him in return and knew he always had their best interests at heart.

Over the next few years, two babies were added to the family. Now they were a family of six.

Life was busy and Lucas looked for a way to ensure each child knew how important they were to him. That's when Daddy Days were started. Each month he would arrange a special day with one of them. The child would get to choose the activity and have their dad's undivided attention for that day. Many memories were created as each child basked in their dad's love.

During this time the girl's biological father still played a role in their lives. Although this man's lifestyle was less than desirable, Lucas didn't speak negatively about him to the girls. Instead, he modelled what a loving, committed man looked like. From his example, they learned how a woman deserved to be treated.

Years passed quickly and the girls became young adults. They were now 18 and 20, old enough to make their own decisions. One night they came to their dad with some paperwork and asked if he'd help them fill it out. They handed Lucas the forms necessary for him to legally adopt them!

Lucas was overjoyed. He had always considered them to be his children. Now they wanted to officially state that they belonged to him.

Papers were filed and the adoption was completed. This formality publicly expressed what had been in their hearts for many years.

The love of an exceptional dad strengthened my granddaughters' sense of self-worth and gave them a firm foundation on which to build their lives. For this I am eternally grateful.

6

A GODLY FATHER'S PRAYERS

BY DUANE SIMS

My dad was a quiet, unassuming man. He was a farmer, a horse enthusiast, a lover of family and family memories, and my Sunday school teacher for a while. He loved God.

I remember a season many years ago, when I was being bullied both at school and on the bus ride to school. I remember him walking me down part of the country road to where the bus picked me up, and then stopping and watching me walk the rest of the way. I would glance back to see if he was still there, and sure enough he was watching me intently. Somehow I knew he was praying for me. Later, my mom told me that he prayed a lot for me.

It's funny, but after he passed away I believe that I could sense that he was no longer there to pray for me. By this time he was over 90 and I was over 50 years of age, but he was still my dad and I was still his boy. Somehow I just knew that there were things in the spiritual sphere that his prayers protected me from.

He would often say that he was proud of my ability to preach the gospel. In his modest and self depreciating fashion, he would say that he could hardly believe that a son of his could preach like that, and yet I knew that I wouldn't be able to do what I did without his quiet example. And in fact some of my early preaching mentors were men that he listened to on the radio and read in print. He and I would sometimes listen to them together over the years.

And now it's my turn to continue to pray for my grown children and grandchildren.

There are moments when I remember his example, as well as recall the strengthening nature of a godly father's prayers.

HOW MY VETERAN LOVES

BY DEACON MINISTER SHARLAE HARRIS

Many people come up with a way that seems right to them about how or what it means to truly love. Coming from a dark place in life, I thought I would never know the real answer to love. I met a man of valour, a man of honour, a veteran man who made a choice to serve not just me or a family but his entire country. Choosing to serve or to be a servant of others is the highest point in life that a person could be. Thank you for your service.

My veteran loves in a way that is so unselfish. He puts others before himself at any cost it seems. He demonstrates his love for me in ways no one has ever done before. He demonstrates a heart of giving and strives for nothing less than seeing a smile on the face of his loved ones. A nudge on the shoulder from a higher power lets him know he is doing a good job.

Every day that this man who is worthy of honour wakes up to see another day to show love, give love, and minister love to whomever he chooses is what gives him strength, courage, and the wisdom to go forward. After all, this is what gives serving its meaning.

This is a man who is an only child of his mother. For him, this is a low point due to the fact of having no siblings to confide in or to share spankings with when growing up as a child. A lot of the teachings growing up can be a lot of weight for one tiny little fellow. Then you become an adult and wow, the mind is blown, and it can get very lonely.

This great man of honour has recently lost his mother. He has shown a tremendous amount of tenacity, bravery, faithfulness, love, gratitude, and more. He is one of the top-rated fathers I have ever known. I cannot tell you how other people feel when they have been impacted by his love, but I can tell you how I witness the impact he has on others. People call on him continuously and no one does that unless there has been a good result/return/impact in their lives. He has been a saviour for me. He is my husband and I know for a fact that God saved his best for me. I have had no down moments or low points brought on by this man. Through sickness, pain, ups and downs, he will always be my man of honour and my veteran love.

In the wake of an absent parent, in the wake of a health scare where it looked like all hope was gone, in the wake of an attack that felt like an ambush, God turned it around and all hope was restored unto him, and that attack became his army. There is more with him than against him. This man (my man) has turned every tragic moment since I have been in his life into a moment of growth and maturity. Just watching him teaches me new strategies, new attitudes of gratitude, how to find the silver linings, new phases of self-control, healings that help people not hurt people, walks, and talks that complement each other, and so many things that I have been able to utilize in my very own life.

The biggest lesson that all of this has taught me in how my veteran loves is how not to be stuck in our own ways. Our own way may not be the best way or the way that we are are intended to follow so we must always be teachable. We are put here on this earth to learn from one another. We are supposed to love our neighbour as we love ourselves and that means to honour.

With all this being said, to my man of honour and all the men of honour of this magnificent piece, you are masterpieces in the earth and there is no greater respect than what we have for you all. Thank you for being so worthy to be marked with greatness. May all the rest of your days be wonderful, peaceful, loving, filled with kindness and all that you have given to the world, to your families, and to yourselves be given back to you pressed down, shaken together, and flowing over coming in and going out. The world is beautiful with you in it and without you the void would be felt.

When we honour someone, it tells the world that they are special and that they have done something that deserves attention brought to the character of who they are. It means that you are enough. It means that you are worthy of notability. It gives who you are a definition to be spoken about that can transition and save lives. When you are a prominent person in the world or in the lives of your family and friends it means that your word is valuable, and you can be trusted and counted on. This man of honour can be trusted to fight for me. If you are listed or mentioned in this written piece of work, you can be counted on to fight for me. You all have a warrior spirit that cannot be ripped away from you. You are being counted in the number to birth winners and more men of honour into the world. Keep doing what you are doing. No matter who sees or doesn't see, it is working, and you have more giants slayed than not. I love you; we love you and celebrate you. My man of honour is Donzell C. Harris. Your legacy will live on!

WALTER KITTLER

BY SHEILA WEBSTER

When I was younger, I had a friend who was about forty years older than me.

He used to be a conductor for CN railroad. He, like many railroaders, had a siding named after him. Walter was interesting for that reason and so many more.

Sometimes I would go for coffee early in the morning at The Whistle Stop with him and his friend Jim who was an engineer with CN.

Walter would talk about hunting and fishing, church, his family, railroading, relationships — the sky was the limit really.

He was married for over fifty years maybe sixty — he had a lot of wisdom.

We would tell jokes, puns, talk about the neighbours and ourselves.

He loved being a conductor so much that after he retired, he stayed in shape and worked on a tourist train. He did this I think until the year before he passed away in his eighties.

He talked about meeting the Dixie Chicks one time on the train and what a good group of girls they were.

Another time they used the tourist steam train in the movie *Legends of the Fall*, and you can briefly see him conducting.

He loved that era of life. He met Brad Pitt and Anthony Hopkins. Walter said Anthony Hopkins was a 'real gentlemen and a regular guy.'

"He would ask us about our lives and was interested, not fake."

Walter would talk about the love of his life, his wife Alice, his kids, grandkids, and I think great grandkids by that time. It was so refreshing to hear someone married so long still be enthusiastic about it.

Walter volunteered around town and helped lots of people. He was still always up for coffee early in the morning, then mid-morning at the seniors' center and again at 2:30!

He died full of life and helping. He had just finished counting the offering at church, as he was an usher. He said he didn't feel well and had to go home right then.

His wife found him at home, passed away from a heart attack.

I wrote a poem once based on him and Jim's coffee times with me as a young mom at the time.

It was called, "The Company of Old Men."

9

MY ADOPTED BROTHER

BY MARY ANNE FOCHT

I didn't have many models of good males when I was growing up.

My father at this point is unknown. My stepfather was horribly abusive. My brother would probably have been fine if it wasn't for the example of my stepfather and his abuse of my brother.

So, then my brother did some of the same things as my stepfather when he got older.

My grandpa was good, and I thought of him as more of a friend because he was willing to play cards with me.

My grandpa died though when I was 13. He died on Christmas Day.

I was traumatized by that time because my brother was missing, then murdered, and then my mom died, and I went to live with my oldest sister's adoptive mom.

I didn't talk much the first six months.

By my 21st birthday I had started to notice how kind Joel was. He helped his wife clean the house, never yelled, or got mad.

This past May we stayed over at his house, and he got up in the morning and made us all (8 of us and then his family) breakfast, not just his wife. Then he changed his toddler and baby's diapers and clothes for church.

He left and helped with lights at church before we all got there. That was amazing.

10

MY BEST FRIEND

BY SHEILA WEBSTER

There is a man, who I don't call by name even though I believe it is important to call people by their names.

I do this out of respect because he is a private person and sometimes my enthusiasm about what a good friend he is, is well a little much for such a humble and unassuming person.

There are so many reasons that he is a wonderful person and I am blessed to have him as a friend. Our friendship may not meet the requirements of traditional thought on equals, but it works and that is what matters.

Some of his qualities are that he is such a thorough and thoughtful worker, conscientious and grace filled when others are not quite as conscientious. Even though our village has an assortment of jobs, he had to take one that was minimum wage. In the years he has worked at it, I have never heard him complain about his work, colleagues or bosses. I have worked with men all my life and aside from a few others of a generation above me I have never seen this before. He wouldn't have had to do another thing I don't think to earn my respect!

As a single mom, it is huge if a man of quality is careful and considerate when he notices the children I raise and doesn't override our house rules. Not only is this man like that he has gone above and beyond in ways few men do.

He taught five of my kids to snowboard in one day and paid for it then took us for supper! It was an amazing gift of generosity, time, kindness and selflessness. My kids still talk about it well into the summer what a perfect day it was for them.

People don't realize how kids without a significant other adult person in their life soak up and drink in each moment and unwrap the experience again and again. Makes sense though, we do it as adults and call it cherished memories. With kids though it sinks deep into them. Later as they reflect on those moments they try and model behaviour they admire in a person who is older.

There are so many little things he does that add up to an incredible wealth and depth of good character and a fine person.

But as my friend he has changed my life in a way education and other friendships have not.

He is consistent with his own beliefs but does not put others down for theirs and is respectful about it. I find this a truly amazing quality in a man in this era we find ourselves in. When there is so much bashing of political alignments, gender and beliefs on social media and in person I have found his stability and kindness like an anchor.

Personally, my life totally crashed during our friendship, and he has assured me on several occasions that I do not have to hide how bad things are for me, he is not weak and can handle even negative emotions. Through that strength I have been able to recover to be better than I ever was in all sectors.

Of course, I am smart enough to know that I do have a foundation of education, years of spiritual maturity, and other building blocks that his friendship and time commitment added to. However, after two failed marriages and many complex friendships his place in my life was different and his friendship the model and the lifeline that cemented me together.
 His stability, even during his own life turbulences was what changed my

internal life and external expression of myself.

Life is perhaps more complex and challenging than it has been in the past few decades, but simplicity brings us back to centre and sanity and that is a huge thing for a friendship to offer.

A simple board game, orange juice, sharing thoughts, movies, popcorn, drives, music, sunsets, a listening ear, wisdom, simple experiences. He offers these with consistency, generosity and says no when he cannot for his own reasons.

He is a lover of nature and connects as well as engages with it in a deep way. I love his creativity and artistic endeavours, whether in music or art. He is confident enough to encourage me to exceed my own current level of performance, but smart enough to tell me when I am too hard on myself.

It takes some people a master's level course to know how to ask and use the right questions, and he does. He can drive a point home to be in five to ten words, with kindness and redemption in a way I have never see anyone else able to – which makes him not only empathetic but incredibly wise.

He may see himself as an ordinary man, but in mine and the children's eyes he is a slayer of dragons, fun factory, and a man who has our respect and love.

11

MORE THAN READING, WRITING, AND ARITHMETIC

BY RUTH L. SNYDER

Silver-haired Mr. Arthur Freeman often greeted us with a twinkle in his eye and a smile on his lined face. He exemplified the characteristics he expected in his grade 7 classroom — discipline, hard work, respect, and kindness.

Along with the usual struggles of a twelve year old, I faced the adjustment of moving from the third-world culture I had enjoyed in Botswana, Africa, to the first-world culture of rural western Canada. Mr. Freeman gently guided me, encouraged me, and challenged me. Along with the required curriculum, he often served up stories from his life. He told us about challenges he faced, like parenting his kids who chose to rebel and leave home, but eventually restored their relationships with him. He shared failures and victories. He urged us to make good choices.

Starting the year I was in grade 7 and continuing until after I finished my post secondary education, Mr. Freeman sent me a birthday card with a bookmark and a personal handwritten note in the mail. I discovered he sent these birthday greetings to every student he ever had in his classroom.

When I was an adult, my respect and appreciation for him multiplied. I phoned him to confess I had cheated on a test in one of his classes. He graciously thanked me for phoning, offered his forgiveness, and told me he was proud of me. Then he reminded me to make good choices.

Mr. Robert Rougeau taught me band and Bible during my grade 10 year. At first his rigid behaviour puzzled me. Then I discovered he served as a member of the Royal Canadian Mounted Police. I made it my goal to make him smile. Every time I entered his classroom or passed him in the hallway, I did or said something funny. It took a few weeks, but eventually he smiled when he saw me.

Although Mr. Rougeau seemed serious most of the time, he did have a sense of humour. We attended high school on the campus of Prairie Bible College. At that time, the college hosted an annual conference focused on missions, held in a massive building called the Prairie Tabernacle, which has since been demolished. The college invited our band to perform before one of the many services held that week. One of the pieces we performed was Sheep May Safely Graze by J.S. Bach. During our performance, half of our band played the piece in cut time (as was marked on the music), and half played in 4/4. Mr. Rougeau made no indication anything was wrong during our performance, although I'm sure he was terribly embarrassed. At our next rehearsal he told us he would be referring to the piece as Sheep May Munch and we all had a good laugh together.

Mr. Rougeau and I had some great discussions about the Bible. He was a fairly new Christian compared to me, but he studied diligently and taught me to appreciate tools like *Strong's Concordance* and he also encouraged me to read from different translations to get a fuller understanding. He challenged me to ask questions instead of just agreeing with everything I heard or had been previously taught.

I didn't hear from Mr. Rougeau often after he moved back to British Columbia to work with the RCMP. However, we did keep in touch. He told me he was excited that I had decided to attend Bible college. Halfway through my first year, he phoned me. He asked what I was learning and how I was doing. Then, he asked if I had enough money to pay for my year in college. I told him I had been amazed at how God had provided, but I was still a bit short. He directly asked me how much I needed.

When I told him, he replied, "I will put a cheque for $800 (the amount I still owed) in the mail tomorrow." He did what he said, and also sent me several study tools.

Mr. Graeme Crouch taught me several courses throughout Bible College. He was also our class supervisor in our first year. Mr. Crouch came to Canada from Australia to attend Bible College and then joined staff. Although his accent had gentled over the years, it was obvious where he grew up.

Mr. Crouch had high expectations of us as students. The multiple pages of notes I took in his class left my fingers cramped. He amused and exhorted us through his descriptive stories. Although he dealt with hundreds of students, he had a way of making me feel like he saw each student had time time for us.

One day Mr. Crouch called me to his office. He greeted me cheerfully and asked how I was doing. Nominations were open for positions had other students had nominated me for two different positions. I was unaware that the two positions conflicted time-wise with each other. Mr. Crouch patiently explained the responsibilities of each of the positions and why it would not be possible for me to fulfill both of them.

He asked me which position I would rather let my name stand for. I responded. He told me that no one other than the two of us would be aware of my nomination for the second position. Then he made a statement that has guided me since. "Ruth, remember that you cannot do anything to make God love you more. Neither can you do anything to make God love you less. God loves you completely because he chooses to love you."

I'm grateful for these three godly men who taught me more than reading, writing, and arithmetic.

THE COMPANY OF MEN
BY SHEILA WEBSTER

I miss the company of old men,
The ones who who still work
Whose sweat smells like hard sun
Who smoke a pipe
Whose scent mingles with elements

They will sit in a coffee shop
And spin stories
And pull a chair out
For a lady
Then argue over who pays
For coffee
Today and tomorrow

Men who talk of years ago

THE COMPANY OF MEN

As if it were yesterday
They remember the girl
Who stole their heart
50 years ago
But are still married to the
Same wife

Men who hunt and fish
And tell stories
Not only of the
One that got away
But they have pictures
Of those that didn't

Men who laugh about life
The mistakes they made
Who know jokes
Even if they don't get them right

I miss the company of men
Who cry when babies are born
When their friends die
Those who shed a tear when
the caboose disappeared
When an elevator is torn down

MEN WHO MATTER

Men who have time
To sit and talk
And not run away
Men who are 70 and 80
And still full of life
Men who tip
For a cup of coffee

Men who are generous
Because that's the way to be
Who are courageous
Even when they are quaking
Who are courteous
But would be the first to defend

I felt full and rich
Work was worth doing
And life worth living
When I was in the company
Of old men....

13

MY DAD WAS ALWAYS THERE FOR ME

BY ASHLEY CARROLL

During my growing up years, my dad was a man of few words, but no matter what, he was always there for me. Like when I had to make the scary phone call to tell him I rolled his car. It was the longest ten minutes of my life as I waited for my parents to pick me up. I dreaded the trouble I thought I would be in for speeding and wrecking the car. He just hugged me and was glad I was okay.

Another time, I thought I would put washer fluid in the car—only it ended up going where the coolant should go...oops! I had to drive to write a university exam the next day and was feeling kind of stressed.

MY DAD WAS ALWAYS THERE FOR ME

My dad siphoned the washer fluid and fixed everything for me!

Other memories, like the pride he showed when I graduated from high school and university. Other times when I was making decisions that weren't so great, like poor relationship choices or financial decisions, he was always there to offer guidance. Even when I thought I knew more and didn't need to follow his advice he was still always there for me. Always there to pick me up when things went south.

When I moved to Alberta by myself for a teaching position my dad was the person I would call, in tears, feeling so homesick I wanted to go back home. I'm sure I called every day for probably two weeks straight. Each time he talked me down and reminded me I had never quit anything in my life so why would I now. He encouraged me that I could get through it and I did. Now I've called Alberta home for thirteen years!

When I got married, my dad was so proud that I found a man who respected and loved me for who I was. A year after I got married, I was diagnosed with cervical cancer and had a hysterectomy. I felt like my world was crashing in around me. Although my husband stood by my side for all of this and was the best support I could ever imagine, I felt like I was letting people down, like our family and our parents. I felt like I was inadequate and denying them grandchildren, although this thought was only in my mind, not theirs. My dad was there for me—doing little things like mowing my lawn and helping to get a vehicle issue dealt with while I was healing. It's always the little things he does that may not come out as words that mean the most.

Later on when my husband was laid off from his job and started his own business my dad was always there to offer advice, even helping us to pay bills when we were financially drowning. He helped to make the decision to get rid of the business when it was deeply affecting our mental health. He helped us realize taking care of ourselves—both our physical and mental health—was more important than succeeding with a business.

When my niece and nephew were born, he never missed a moment of their lives watching every sports game and being there for every special moment. In the past few years, my dad has taught me through the simple act of just being there that family is most important.

14

MY TEACHER

BY ZANDER BRADLEY - AGE 16

At first, I thought he was kinda lame. I'm in grade ten and I thought he was just rule-abiding kinda stuff.

Then halfway through first semester I talked to him a bit more and I thought he was more chill.

When our class was on a ski/snowboarding trip I got to hang out with him a bit more and he was more than cool.

He was really fun and like a different person. More relaxed, hyper, like a kid-in-a-candy-shop kinda excited.

He was not just good at snowboarding; he was really good! We hung out most of the day on the hill and it was awesome.

Since then, he has been kinda just cool with me when I screwed up at school a couple times.

I hope I graduate in a couple years and even if I don't go to same school that he can come to my grad.

15

MEN I ADMIRE

BY LUKE SNYDER

My dad is a good hunter and leader. He tells me about the Lord.

I like going fishing, setting traps, and playing with Buddy, our mutt, with Dad.

Uncle Tim lets me play with LEGO when we are at his place. I appreciate that he doesn't use God's name in vain.

Grandpa Beam had lots of stories to tell. I appreciated his good looks and natural talents. He was one of the oldest, wisest people of God I knew. He's up in Heaven now.

16

TODD MAGNUS

BY MARY ANNE FOCHT

Some men don't realize just by being who they are they make a big impact.

I did not have a good life growing up and did not know what I was going to be able to do.

When I came to live with Sheila it took a lot to get me to a place where I realized I had to do things for myself, like clean. I was in deep trauma.

Sheila finally encouraged me to move out on my own because I was an adult even though I was what they call trauma-delayed.

A kind person, Todd Magnus, let me rent his trailer in our village for not very much money. It was fun at first to be on my own, but things didn't always go the way Sheila hoped they would.

For me, though, it was amazing to have a place of my own. I felt safe and I started to heal in that trailer because it was my own space. I could control my space; who came-and-went, and it felt safer. I learned how much I didn't know about life.

Todd didn't hassle Sheila when she had to advocate for things like an extension on rent.

Sheila tried to explain finances to me as she would pay for whatever I couldn't afford or was covered by social services. I am sure it was harder on her than I ever will know.

Todd and his wife were very nice to rent to me for so long as I had wanted to buy it and had been promised a small inheritance from my grandma's death. However, it was too long of a court process and Sheila said she couldn't afford to subsidize my dream there anymore.

I was really sad to leave my first adult home, but appreciated how kind Todd had been to me. If he had not rented to me, I don't know if I could have gotten as far in life as I have.

I hope he knows how much appreciated a safe place and his kindness.

17

IT'S HOW YOU FINISH

BY TRACY KRAUSS

My father was many things. Tall, handsome, athletic, persuasive, and possibly the best salesman to walk the earth. He also had a very sensitive and empathetic side which, unfortunately, was sometimes inappropriately directed. But honourable? That was not a word anyone would have used to describe my father for the first three quarters of his life.

My dad was "illegitimate," born to a widow with six other children at a time when such a thing was out-and-out scandalous. His biological father was her farm hand, hired after her husband's death. My paternal grandfather also had other children, and apparently, he drank, so they never did get together. The story goes that when my dad was a small boy, Granny sent the hired man packing and my dad never spoke to him again, even though they lived in the same small town. He did maintain a relationship with his father's other children, but he just couldn't forgive his father. Did I mention stubborn in my list of descriptors? My dad was that and then some. He could hold a grudge with the best of them.

His whole life Dad had to fight for respect. He was whispered about, taunted at school, many other kids weren't allowed to socialize with him... So, to say he had something to prove in life was an understatement.

Dad went on to be a star athlete and as I already mentioned, he was a very good-looking man, so when he started dating one of the county's beauties, (a.k.a my mother – she and her sister were known as "The Miller girls" and were quite the catch) he should have been satisfied. But he wasn't. His need to prove his worth led him to all kinds of entrepreneurial endeavors, some more successful than others, and a whole lot of moving from house to house. By the time I left home, I had moved fifteen times.

Unfortunately, he also had a wondering eye. In his defense, his affairs (he had more than one) stemmed from his need to rescue women from abusive relationships. He became their champion, but inevitably, as can happen, close proximity led to other things. As the youngest of five, my entire childhood was clouded by the unhappy state of my parents' marriage. Finally, after too many years of "staying together for the children" my parents got a divorce.

I don't want to paint a totally bad picture of my father because he was still my hero as a little girl. He was kind and caring; he loved his children deeply and I think he was truly sad about how he was hurting all of us—even Mom. I believe he never stopped loving her, even though he was unfaithful. Despite his weaknesses and struggles, I was always proud of him. I knew how much he cared for me. I was his little princess.

At this point I must tell you a bit about my mother. She was a vibrant, sometimes flamboyant, artistic type. When she came to Christ, she was ALL IN. As a teenager, I was embarrassed at times, believe me! She was fervent in her prayers, and even through all the years that my parents were divorced, she continued to pray for my father's salvation.

Sometime in his late sixties my father had a mild heart attack. He did not need surgery, but it was obviously a wakeup call. He left his then girlfriend and moved back in with my mom. The first time they came to visit us together, my eldest daughter was perplexed. She was around seven at the time and had never seen her grandparents together before. She said, "Mommy! Grandpa and Grandma are here. Together!" My siblings and I used to joke that our parents were "living in sin" since they were technically not married anymore!

I am not entirely certain when Dad gave his life to Christ, but it was sometime after the events that came next. Only a few years after my parents reunited, my mother got dementia. Her mind went very quickly as she progressed from pleasant confusion to all out silence. Through those years before her death, my father became the husband she had been had praying for and that she deserved. Even once she had to be placed in a nursing home, he faithfully went every day to feed her and care for her. It was heart wrenching and touching, to say the least.

My mother's prayers were answered. I know she prayed for his salvation—no matter what it would take, and I believe she would have willingly given up her own life and sanity if it meant he would come to Christ. In the end, that's what happened. He had finally become that man of honour.

True to form, after Mom's passing, Dad took up with a lovely Christian widow whom he'd met in the nursing home. Once a ladies' man, always a ladies' man, I guess.

(Did I mention how handsome he was? Even as an old man, he was so handsome!) This time, however, he was free to be with someone else, and his faith soared. For someone who had never been overtly spiritual or demonstrative in his faith, his love for Jesus came shining through in those latter years.

He and his new lady friend had five good years together until he died of cancer at 85. She and my sister had the privilege of singing him into heaven, since he wouldn't go to a hospital. (Stubborn right to the end, too!) His eyes lit up and he reached for heaven as he took his last breath.

It brings a tear to my eye, even now, so many years later, as I think about my parents' reunion in heaven. I can imagine my mother, whirling in the arms of her prince as they dance together on those streets of gold, his eyes locked on hers and shining with love. No more shame. No more guilt. Just the pure, unadulterated love that only Jesus can give.

18

MITCH OSIOWY

The first time we met Mitch it was before 8 o'clock in the morning at our new home.

All the kids in town were taking each other's bikes and riding them but somehow, he thought we stole them.

He banged on our door so hard we thought it was the cops.

My mom was already crying because my new sister had done something really bad. Us kids weren't listening and had been yelling at her.

For a second you could tell she wanted him as a man to understand her situation, but he wasn't listening. He told her to do better and there would be trouble if me and Zander ever took his kids bikes again period. I don't think my mom ever got over how much that shook her up.

Over the years I understood that he was just looking out for his own kids.

He was amazing as a single dad taking care of his own four kids. Us kids all wished someone looked out for our mom and us like he did for his kids.

Joshua Heath - Age 21

The first time I saw Mitch was a week after I came to live with my Aunty. I was out for a bike ride. He is First Nations, and he did a peace sign at me.

I played with his son Joe sometimes at school and occasionally David but not the older kids.

Sometimes he would play with us at the park and it made me very happy that a First Nations man would take time for me.

We moved closer to him in the trailer park and every time he saw us, he would give us the peace sign.

I felt like he liked me a lot and it made me happy.

I was very, very, very sad when he died. I felt like his kids were a million times sadder than me so that made me even sadder.

I didn't want to stay in school because the thought of him dying, it made me so sad because I couldn't explain what he meant to me.

Mitch was a good dad and it's sad to see his kids shooting baskets at their house without him to laugh with and teach them.

Dallas - age ten

I saw Mitch when I first moved here. It made me happy when he did the peace sign cuz I thought he was cool.

He was very nice to his kids, and I wish my dad was nice like that and didn't teach his kids bad things.

I was very sad when he died but proud of his kids talking about him at the funeral.

Ares - age seven

I saw Mitch play with his kids, and they loved him.

His girl is beautiful, and I love her hair.

I wish he didn't die. His kids loved him. We miss him.

Tessie age 5

THREE MEN I ADMIRE

BY JOSHUA HEATH

There are three men I admire.

Steven - He is Indigenous like me so that is cool.

He has gone through some of the same stuff as me like drugs and anger so that helps me understand I can change.

He is funny, kind, brave, and works hard. I like that he loves his kids and tries to be there for them — I never had that growing up.

I like watching him spend time with my mom and make her laugh and he calls her a friend. He is really kind to the kids we are raising and a good example.

Ben - He is a hard worker and doesn't complain like I do. He isn't embarrassed to say hi to us in our town.

He has made my mom's life easier by encouraging her that she is a good person and not a failure. He never makes her feel bad.

Ben taught us to snowboard this year and it was amazing to have a man teach us something and he paid for snowboarding and supper. My mom still cries about how generous and kind that was because most people don't know how hard it is to raise us kids without a strong man in our life and we take things out on her that aren't her fault.

Ben is nice to the little kids in our family and gives them hugs sometimes which they need. I didn't get that growing up from a man, so I know what it means to them.

Joel became my brother when I was adopted. He works hard and helps everybody.

He shows us new things and is a great person as a brother. He is funny and tells us about his jobs.

I feel bad for the things I stole from him when I was younger, but he forgave me.

He is a good husband and father and takes care of his family. He is sick but still he always has a good attitude and even cooks and cleans and changes diapers.

Joel is one of the best men I have ever met in my life — maybe the best.

20

A HUSBAND OF CHARACTER

BY SALLY MEADOWS

My husband Jeff was a firstborn, and like many firstborns, he was responsible, goal oriented, hardworking, stubborn, creative, and a perfectionist. Even as a young teen, he excelled at whatever he put his hand to, from academics to sports to the many artistic endeavours he pursued including music, art, building model ships, and painting historical figurines.

I met Jeff during my first year of graduate studies. I was in the lab reviewing microscope slides for an upcoming tutorial when I glanced up to see a handful of students slinking single file across the room, gawking at the new female tutorial assistant. I recognized a few of the students from my class and waved a greeting. Caught red-handed, they sheepishly strolled over to where I was sitting, where I was introduced to the young man who would change my life forever.

I started spotting Jeff doing homework at one of the communal desks just inside the entrance to the campus building where I regularly parked my bicycle. He always stood up and greeted me as I entered. Call me naïve, but it took a while before it dawned on me that it wasn't coincidence that he "happened" to be doing homework at the same time and place I arrived for work every morning.

Women like to be wooed and woo me Jeff did. His friendly, smiling face won me over, and it wasn't long until he asked me out. Our first date, at the apartment I shared with two other students, was watching the movie *Greystoke: The Legend of Tarzan, King of the Apes* on video. Less than 20 minutes into the movie, he slowly swivelled my chair towards him, gently took my bare feet in his hands, placed them on his lap, and gave me a foot rub. I was smitten. It was an evening ritual he repeated many times over our 34 years of marriage. (Lucky me!)

As our relationship grew, I was attracted to Jeff's ability to easily engage others in conversation. (Later I realized that it didn't come naturally to him but was something he worked at because it was important to him.) He was polite and considerate, and clearly valued others and their thoughts and feelings. He always treated people well, putting them first, even when they didn't extend the same courtesy.

There was a purity about Jeff that really spoke to my heart. He was a kind, gentle, thoughtful man who loved nature. His beautiful spirit shone when interacting with animals of all kinds. He had an astounding breadth of knowledge about the natural world—the rocks, trees, birds, and wildlife—and was highly influential to me, as a self-proclaimed "indoor person," coming to appreciate and love the great outdoors through our many hikes together. When we got married, one of our friends laughingly commented that she had never heard anyone say "I do" more confidently than me.

Jeff had a softness about him that lent itself well to being a parent, even though early on, I'm sure he was a bit shell shocked. When he lost his job eight months after our second was born and I had to go back to work, he never complained about having to stay home and take care of two little ones. In fact, Jeff rarely complained about anything. Whatever life threw our way, he stepped up regardless of personal cost or disappointment.

Jeff was a conscientious worker and had great pride in being able to provide for his family throughout most of our married life, despite a few hard knocks at the beginning and end of his career. He worked diligently and was eventually rewarded with a successful long-time career with a mining company. He had an incredible sense of style and wore a suit well. Because of his artistic streak, he was not shy in playing with bright shirt and tie colours and patterns to personalize his conservative suits, despite the teasing by his co-workers. He was proud to get dressed up and go to work every day with a company that had an excellent reputation both internally and in the industry.

Throughout our married life—and in fact, since we got engaged—Jeff showed his commitment to the Lord, and to growing in his faith. He was always eager to learn about spiritual matters, and even more eager to share. Over the years, he served as a small group leader; played the drums on countless worship teams and at special events; and occasionally preached. He had a servant heart and was willing to help wherever needed, whether at church, outreach events, or as a volunteer at food banks. He often worked behind the scenes, no matter how "lowly" the task was. Despite working full time, he also pursued a Bachelor of Theology, graduating in 2020. Like King David, he truly was a man after God's heart.

A HUSBAND OF CHARACTER

Like all of us, Jeff had his weaknesses and personal challenges. Nonetheless, he tried to do the very best he could as a husband, father, employee, neighbour, son, and ministry leader. When he passed away suddenly in 2022, many people came forward to share stories about his kindness, humbleness, sensitivity, and his quirky sense of humour.

For me, the true character of a man—what assigns him honour—is how he treats others. To Jeff, it didn't matter what someone's station in life was, their economic situation, the colour of their skin, their gender, and whether they were old or young or somewhere in between; he always showed value and respect to everyone he encountered.

A few weeks before Jeff passed, I shared with him that the Lord had put the importance of legacy on my heart. Sadly, we never fully discussed what that meant to us individually and as a couple. But that's okay; because of who he was and the impact he had on family, friends, and countless others; his legacy is clear. So, as I move forward alone in life and ministry on behalf of both of us, I pray that the Lord gives me the strength, wisdom, and courage to remember and carry on the very best of my husband; and that I do it with the grace, generosity, and kindness he so aptly modelled.

21

JOSIA

BY SHEILA WEBSTER

My daughter fell hard for a man that met most of her must haves for a future partner. He loved dancing, castles, *Lord of the Rings*, board games, and shared her faith. The challenge — he had only lived in our country a few short weeks before their meeting.

They captured each other's hearts from the first night and were engaged a scant six weeks later, and married six weeks after that.

They quickly made a lovely home and did many amazing things including going to Germany to see the castles near his home.

He always tries to be respectful even when he doesn't agree and has worked at jobs he hates, made sure they paid off student loans, there is always food in their home, fun for their kids and many friends, young and old alike.

I admire so many things about him and my daughter for the life they have built in a short time through a lot of hardships.

Josia is one of a kind and I am very happy to know him and glad that we continue to work on our relationship.

22

THINGS I LIKE TO DO WITH MY DAD

BY DANE - AGE 5

I like blowing bubbles with my dad. I also like going to the city with him. I got to do that when I finished my sticker chart. We go to the dump together. A long time ago we went to the drive-in movie theatre. I don't remember what movie we saw.

My dad gives me things like popsicles and says I can have some snacks. He buys me chips! My dad gives me all kinds of toys.

I love my dad.

23

A FATHER OF MANY TALENTS

BY JEWELL VANSTONE

Being a parent is never easy as I think most adults with children will agree. After they are born, we begin to bond with them and with further development we begin seeing their personalities. This process is different with adults joining a family later in life. How this merger takes place is dependent on many factors such as the personality and age of all parties.

I have seen families with teens join with a new partner of a bio parent come together with excellent and positive results. On the other hand, I have been involved with families where it was not a happy blending. Again, there are so many factors but the disruption of a family unit is always painful and upsetting.

In my case, my son was only fifteen months old when I married for a second time. He would not remember his bio father who passed away at the age of 30 leaving my 6-month-old son and I alone after less than 3 years of marriage. Sorrow and grief do not proffer the best parenting and at the age of 24, I was terrified at the thought of being a single parent. I had actually never lived alone before going from my parents' home to marriage immediately after completing nursing college.

When Tyler was 11 months old he became very ill and required emergency surgery while we were visiting my parents and so he spent time in the Moose Jaw hospital thus keeping me there as well. As I took some time to myself, I wandered the mall a bit and bumped into a friend. Since being mostly alone I invited him to go out for coffee that evening. He seemed surprised but agreed. He told me later that he knew I was recently widowed and would never have felt it appropriate to ask me out but since I asked, it opened the door. After a bit of reminiscing and catching up we fell into a rhythm of asking and answering questions. Tim doing most of the questioning as was his method of conversation.

Following Tyler's discharge, we returned home to Saskatoon and life carried on. A package arrived in the mail before his first birthday from Tim. A tiny pair of leather cowboy boots! A few phone calls became regular calls and then a date in Saskatoon. Our relationship was a bit awkward at times because of my own feelings of uncertainty but I found his tender care impossible to disregard. We began talking of a more serious relationship and plans for the future. Since I knew my first husband wanted me to find a new partner, even at my dismay, it freed me to consider the possibility. I was feeling uncertain and fearful of giving my heart to another. As we talked about the idea of getting married Tim told me that a farmer can only take time off during winter and that November to March would be the best time for him. We agreed that after harvest that year might be good and left it at that. After a time with God at a retreat I was attending, God told me very clearly that I should marry Tim soon and not wait until fall. This put me into a tailspin because it was so clear and undeniable that I couldn't ignore it. When I got home the next day I phoned him right away and told him that if it was ok with him we should get married before seeding started! As shocked as I was, I felt completely at peace. We picked a date, and I bought a dress. Our parents were aware of our plans and my mom and dad agreed to keep Tyler. We eloped, got married and took off on a honeymoon and I am not sure which of us was more nervous.

And just like that we were a family. Tim brought up changing Tyler's surname even before the wedding and I had thought I wanted to merge his names together. As soon as we were settled Tim urged me to proceed with the legal paperwork and I resisted. It felt like I would be removing part of our history somehow.

Tim really showed his care for Tyler's best interest with his explanation. He said that since we wanted to have more children, if Tyler's name was not the same it would always seem like there was a division between them. Even in school children would be aware of some difference in our family dynamic and that could cause our son to feel somehow separated. Our son – Tim really loved him and wanted to be his dad. As I considered these things, I had to agree that it would be best to start things off together as a family, with a family name.

The anniversary of Abe 's death came around 3 months after we were married. I was not prepared for the huge roller coaster of emotions that this would create. No one warned me this would happen. It was during this time that Tim again showed his tender love for me. He told me that he knew I would always love Tyler more than him and I would never forget my first love, but we would make our own new memories as a family. There are not many men who could take their place in a widow's life so beautifully and not feel jealous at all. It was a beautiful thing.

When I struggled with being ok if Tim disciplined, he found a way to help me share the weight of parenting and trust that he held my heart. I had promised Abe's mother that I would always keep in touch with her and make sure Tyler saw her regularly. Tim was so very good to her and always made sure that we made it happen. When 3 more children were added to our family, Tim always thought of Tyler first just like a first-born child. When things got difficult during the teen years and Tyler questioned how life would have been different if his birth father would have been around, a few things really hurt Tim's feelings. Somehow, he did not dwell on it and loved Tyler through it.

With two sons and two daughters our house was full. Tim and I loved watching them develop, each so unique. A few times there were girls added to our family for a time because of bad home situations or needs we could accommodate. Again, Tim was a faithful father and prayer warrior, modelling gentleness and tender care.

At all times Tim has shared with parenting and decision making. He taught our children to pray about their decisions. He taught them to be thankful in everything. He never left the table without thanking me for the food - even when the meal was simply not great. He always thanked me and in so doing the children all learned the same and I have been so very thankful for that myself.

How can love for a child be born in your heart before you have seen them? Biological parents know this to be true. We love the unborn and yet this man loved my son because he was mine. He took his place as father and dad without question and his love for me crossed all the borders of my heart.

24

JOEL

BY ARES - AGE 7

I love Joel because he is very nice.

He lets me play with his dog and his kids, especially his baby who is cute.

Even though I don't like long drives I don't mind driving to his house.

Joel is nice and I love him. He is nice to his wife and kids and me and only yells at the dog sometimes but not us or his wife.

He makes snacks, supper, takes me on walks with the dog and his kids.

JOEL

He builds things and lets me watch his TV but not bad shows because he doesn't want me to have nightmares.

25

A HEART SON

BY SHEILA WEBSTER

Believe it or not I found a son once. It was February and he was living on and off the streets, couch surfing, living in a cold camper. My heart melted that in this small city anyone would live in these conditions.

Soon he was stopping by after the kids went to school in the morning to eat, warm up and have a quick safe nap.

Some days I would wash his clothes while he slept. He had a lot of anger and some addictions issues, but he was always so kind and respectful to me.

A HEART SON

One day as I was walking the baby in the stroller, he fell in step beside me. We chatted and I asked him why he was so angry.

He stood motionless in the middle of the street. "In all the foster homes, schools, and jails I have been in no one has asked me why I was angry. They just told me to stop." A tear trickled down his handsome face as he told me all the whys.

He became my heart son that day and still is.

One day he wrote me a poem even though he had a low scholastic achievement (about a grade 2 level at 17).

Of all the things I have lost I still wish I had that poem. In it he talked about his life, the world, and what I meant to him. It ended somehow saying, "the only thing wrong with this world is there is not more people like her in it."

I had so many flaws, but his heartfelt message was clear — I meant a lot to him.

Over the years he has never disappointed me. He has always tried to gain knowledge, work hard, show respect, love his kids, and improve in whatever way he can when he understands.

He gets a lot of respect for pulling himself up by his bootstraps with a little help and surviving a challenging upbringing.

I think often of the day he asked me to visit his mom in jail for him as he wasn't allowed to.

His love for his mom no matter what he had been through was evident. I couldn't deny him such a simple request, even though it was hard.

Ian has always had my back and he will always hold a piece of my heart.

26

MY MEMORIES OF DAD

BY RUTH L. SNYDER

I was born in the same hospital as my dad in Battle Creek, Michigan, while my parents were waiting for their visas to go overseas. Six weeks after my birth, my parents took me to South Africa, along with my brothers, Peter, and Paul. We lived close to Johannesburg. Dad worked in the print shop in Roodepoort for South Africa General Mission, along with his friend from Prairie Bible College, Neville Wilkins.

My earliest memories of Dad include our trips to Kruger National Park where we camped and enjoyed photography safaris.

My dad worked as a printer, but photography was one of his passions—taking pictures, developing, and printing them himself. (This was when you had to load film into the camera and use chemicals in a darkroom to develop the black and white pictures.) Since we lived in southern Africa at the time, we were able to go to game parks where animals like lions, giraffe, and crocodiles lived in their natural habitat. Although I didn't enjoy having to sit still for what seemed like hours, I did enjoy watching the images come to life in the dark room. Once, Dad even filled the bathtub with chemicals so that he could develop a large rendition of a glorious African sunset he captured.

Dad introduced me to Gull Lake, Michigan where he grew up when I was five and we were on furlough for a year. He loved to fish, and that year my brothers received fishing poles for their birthdays. They both attended school, but my sister and I were not in school yet. Dad taught us how to put worms on the hook, cast, snag a fish, and reel it in. Many days the two of us would bring home enough fish to feed our family. (We went on many fishing adventures over the years, both in Africa and North America.)

We travelled thousands of miles that year as a family, reporting to the churches and individuals who supported our family. Usually, we stayed in people's homes. Dad was excellent at communicating with his eyes. We learned to watch his eyes for permission when someone asked if we wanted something. We knew we were expected to be always on our best behaviour. I remember the few times we stayed in hotels; Dad would get us checked in and then go to a local rescue mission to see if anyone needed someone to talk with or pray with them.

We moved to Botswana when I was seven. Botswana did not have a lot of infrastructure then, but there was rail service to both South Africa and Rhodesia (now known as Zimbabwe). Most of the roads were not paved, and we came to expect at least one flat tire on every trip we took, because of the prolific thorn trees along the road.

Although Dad was a printer by trade, I think he enjoyed his work in Botswana more. Dad and Mom worked with Pastor Mmolawa and his wife, discipling them and helping them plant a church in both Tonota and Shashe, working with the youth, and ministering to people. Dad enjoyed riding his motorcycle and taught Pastor Mmolawa how to ride as well so they could visit remote areas where the roads were more like trails through the sand and bush.

Botswana is hot, with only two seasons—wet, and dry. The local riverbed was empty during the dry season. During the wet season, Dad would slowly drive the front of our VW Combi into the water flowing in the river. Then he would open his door. If the water stayed out, he knew it was safe to cross the river without flooding the engine of the van. If the water came in, he backed up and we turned around.

One time we wondered how hot it was. Dad put a thermometer outside in the shade and the needle went as far as it could (120 degrees Fahrenheit), so we only knew that it was hotter than that. We grew two gardens every year, because there was only frost a few times a year.

There were lots of snakes around, and all of them were poisonous. Dad made good use of his pellet gun, trying to keep us safe in our yard. Dad worked hard. The Tswana people called him "Big Bull Elephant" because he could carry twice as much as they could, which he demonstrated on a regular basis. We had a lemon tree growing outside our home where the water drained. The lemons grew as large as my dad's hand. He really enjoyed his lemonade! He also drank lots of cold water, and I remember getting in trouble when I forgot to fill up the water pitcher and put it in the fridge.

Dad loved sports of all kinds. In Africa he played tennis as a means of befriending people. One time he entered a tournament in Botswana. When he came home and told Mom, she said, "Do you realize that tournament is sponsored by a liquor company?" Dad decided to participate anyway. He won the tournament, and several bottles of liquor as a prize. As far as we know, he was the only participant who didn't drink alcohol, and everyone knew it. They begged him to give them his prize, but he brought the bottles home and dumped the alcohol down the drain.

Dad enjoyed music. He played an e-flat alto horn and Mom played her accordion. They also sang often. When Dad was walking around and working, he would hum, usually hymns. He knew the words to most hymns by memory. Many people commented about his lovely bass voice.

Back in Canada, Dad served as assistant dean of men at Prairie, alongside Arnold

Olver and Nelson Reid. Many people commented about Dad's big heart, hidden under his somewhat stern exterior. I thought it was strange that people were afraid of my dad! Mom and Dad often hosted Bible College students in our home. Dad loved to tease and laugh and tell stories. He also had many Scripture verses memorized.

As I grew older, I realized that Dad struggled with reading and writing. In school he had been punished for using his left hand, so he learned to write with both hands, in a beautiful flowing script. He also struggled with an undiagnosed learning challenge, and I often heard him call himself "Stupid." He worked twice as hard as most people to learn, but once he learned something, he didn't forget.

When I was in high school, I had the opportunity to spend several Sunday afternoons with my dad. He led a team of college students who were doing door-to-door surveys in Bashaw. On those trips, Dad often talked to me, expressing concern for the people we met, especially the elderly. I remember him saying, "I hope people will remember to come visit me when I grow old."

One cold January day during my second year of Bible College at Prairie, I celebrated my birthday. All I wanted was to go home and see my parents. After classes that day, I supervised a cleaning crew. I finished scrubbing the toilets and put the supplies away. On my way back to check on the rest of the crew, I stopped at a window and stared out at the bleak, snowy landscape. The sidewalk stood empty except for one lone figure in the distance. Something about the person's gait caught my attention. As the individual came closer, a lump grew in my throat. I raced down the stairs, out the door, and into the open arms of my dad. One thing I miss are his hugs.

Dad taught me many things during his life, about loving God, fishing, photography, sports, and serving people. God also taught me some things when dementia stole the man I loved and admired. I was angry and asked God why my dad, who served him so faithfully, had to spend the closing years of his life living in bewilderment and confusion. I shed many tears, grieving the loss of my dad. He spent a couple years in Camrose where I was able to visit him at least every other week. He smiled when I brought some of his favourite treats like Reece's Peanut Butter Cups or ice-cream. The nurses laughed because he always ate his dessert first. Music was the only other way I experienced connection with him. He shuffled to the sitting room with me and sang with his booming bass voice as I played hymns and other songs on the piano. Usually, a group of other residents joined us. Often, they asked me to play a favourite song and smiled and clapped along. One day as I was leaving, I heard God whisper to my heart. "Ruth, have you forgotten that it's not about you, or your dad? Remember the man born blind? It's always about me. It's about glorifying me. There are people in this facility that would never see my love demonstrated if it weren't for your dad being here."

Dad was a saint, but not a perfect man. He had high expectations, and often I felt like I had to be perfect to earn his love. However, I'm grateful I have so many happy memories to hold in my heart and to share with my children, grandchildren, and friends.

27

CLARK DEACON

BY SHEILA WEBSTER

I met a young man a couple years back. He had married a new friend of mine and they were a lovely young couple.

His love for her was evident from the beginning and he was passionate about building a solid life for them.

I watched them evolve as a couple with the normal ups and downs of any newlyweds. He rose to every occasion as a man and that surprised me.

They added an adorable baby girl to their family and through some help he acquired a larger house for his family and growing business.

Clark was a man of many talents and he surprised me one day (reluctantly after being cajoled by his wife) as he could not only sing, but also play the guitar and piano! He was really quite good.

It continually amazed me someone could be so creative and hardworking at such a young age. Clark also makes time for hospitality and practicing his faith with his immediate and extended family.

He is remodelling the house they bought and even though, perhaps at times it doesn't move as quickly as his family wants, he keeps at it.

Honestly, he inspires me to work harder and achieve more in a day.

Not a day goes by that I don't appreciate the gift he is to this world and hope he not only continues to press forward but also finds time to relax.

A few months back they added a second daughter, and he hired a couple employees. At 23 I feel he has accomplished more in a short time than most people at that age!

28

GRANDPAPPA

TESSIE - AGE 5

*E*ven though he isn't my real grandpa, I call him Grandpappa. He is my best friend's grandpa, and she shares him with me.

I love him because he goes outside with us. He watches us play so we don't get hurt.

Grandpappa pretends to throw us way up in the sky and we laugh and laugh.

He has a cat too, named Betsy.

Sometimes he gives me a piggyback or pulls us in the wagon if we have to walk too far.

29

COR HARTENBERG

BY SHEILA SIMS

*C*or was influential in my life because he cared deeply about me in a way few people had. He believed in my academic ability even though I had a slew of not great marks to warrant a different opinion.

I heard him talk, shortly after meeting him, about his life and how he came to Canada. Cor spoke about way the Second World War had affected him, his family and how much the Dutch loved Canadians because of the liberation. Cor loved to speak about his family's experiences during the war at Remembrance Day services because of this.

Over the course of my education, he showed a grit and humanness few men do. He was deeply devoted to his faith, wife, family, and the school.

Cor was the seconder for my oral exam. At the end of my master's degree, I didn't feel I could do it without him. However, just before my oral exam for my first graduate degree, his dad died, his sister died from suicide, and his dear wife had a brain tumour. He asked if he could delay my exam until after his wife's surgery! Who does that? I relieved him of being my seconder.

Sadly, he got cancer shortly before moving back to Ontario. I wanted to see him one last time before he moved even though he wasn't receiving visitors.

I knocked on his door on a sweltering July day, in Moose Jaw, SK. His wife had just stepped out and he came to the door in a white short sleeved dress shirt and his underwear! He grabbed me and kissed me on the forehead, tenderly like you would a small child. No one had done that before or since.

We talked of so many things in a short time knowing it was the last time. When he passed, I sent a quantity of Canadian flag lapel pins for distribution at his funeral to honour him and his love for Canada.

Cor was articulate, funny, passionate and an advocate. At one time they called him the heart of our graduate school and he truly was.

BOOKS COMPILED BY RUTH L. SNYDER & SHEILA WEBSTER

Strong Moms: https://geni.us/StrongMom1

COMING SOON:

- *When Love Isn't Enough: Overcoming Exceptional Challenges*
- *Silent Hope for All Seasons*
- *Courage to Love*
- *Strong Moms Vol 2*
- *Men Who Matter Vol 2*
- *Sunshine & Laughter*

WE WANT TO HEAR FROM YOU!

Connect with us at:

ripplingbrookpress23@gmail.com

If you enjoyed this book, please leave a review on the site you purchased the book from or send it to us at the email above. Thank you for your support!

www.ingramcontent.com/pod-product-compliance
Lightning Source LLC
Chambersburg PA
CBHW071349080526
44587CB00017B/3024